LEPRECHAUN IN THE US!

THE STORY BEHIND THE ST. PATRICK'S DAY CELEBRATION

HOLIDAY BOOK FOR KIDS
CHILDREN'S HOLIDAY BOOKS

D1708264

BABY PROFESSOR

EDUCATION KIDS

Speedy Publishing LLC

40 E. Main St. #1156

Newark, DE 19711

www.speedypublishing.com

Copyright 2017

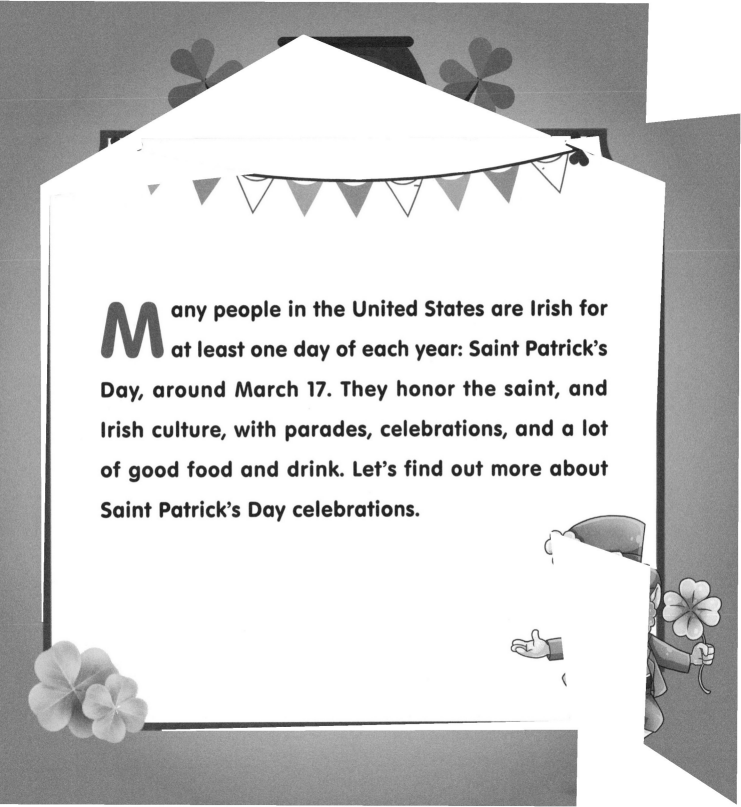

Many people in the United States are Irish for at least one day of each year: Saint Patrick's Day, around March 17. They honor the saint, and Irish culture, with parades, celebrations, and a lot of good food and drink. Let's find out more about Saint Patrick's Day celebrations.

WHO WAS ST. PATRICK?

Patrick, born *Maewyn Succat* somewhere in Britain around 385 CE, became a Christian missionary in Ireland and is credited with spreading the Good News of Jesus Christ in that land. He had many adventures, including being kidnapped by raiders when he was sixteen.

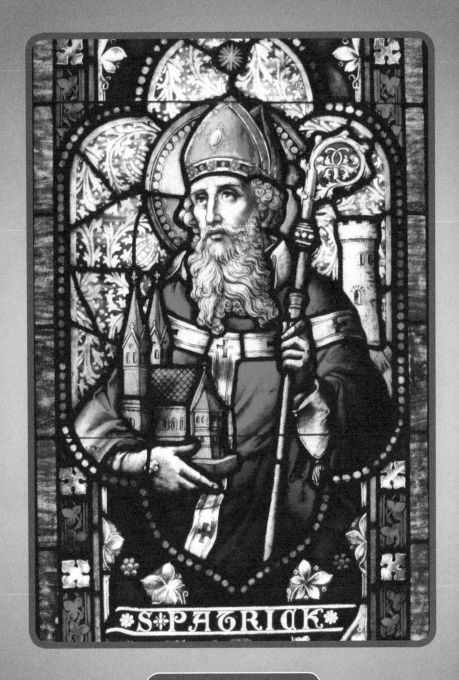

ST. PATRICK

DRUID FOLLOWERS

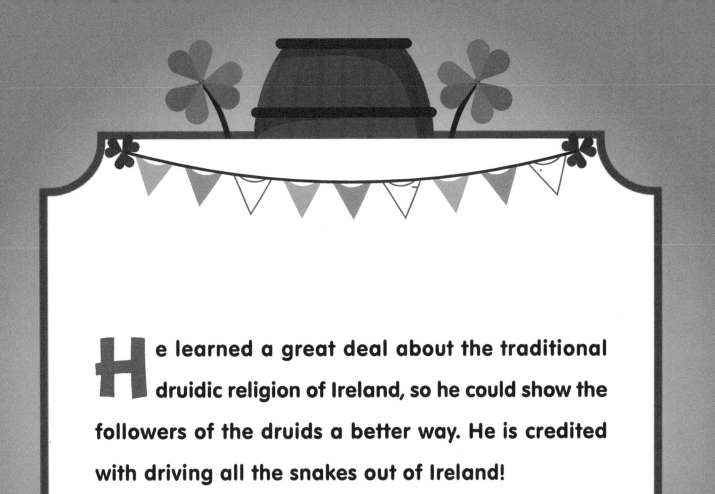

He learned a great deal about the traditional druidic religion of Ireland, so he could show the followers of the druids a better way. He is credited with driving all the snakes out of Ireland!

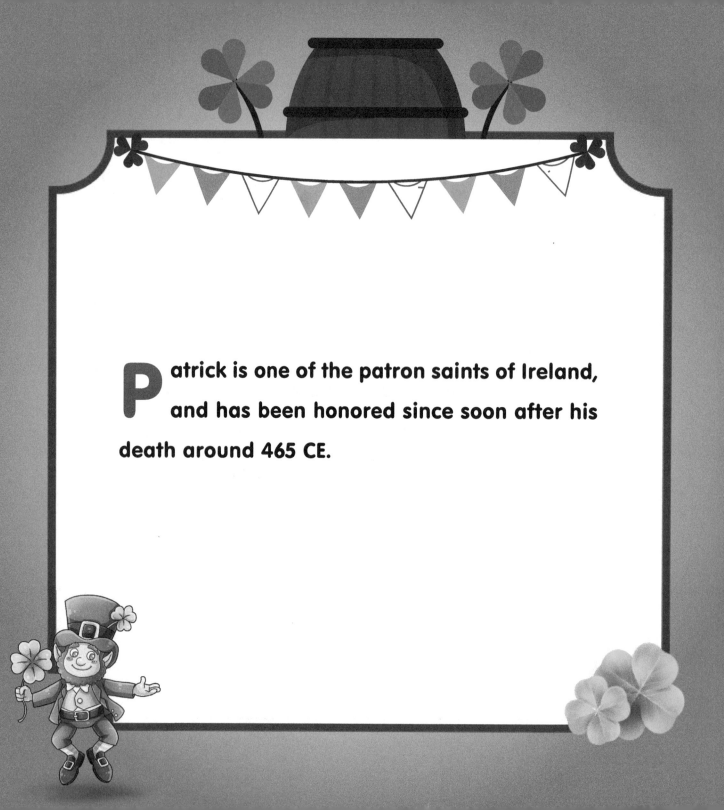

Patrick is one of the patron saints of Ireland, and has been honored since soon after his death around 465 CE.

ST. PATRICK CASTING OUT SNAKES

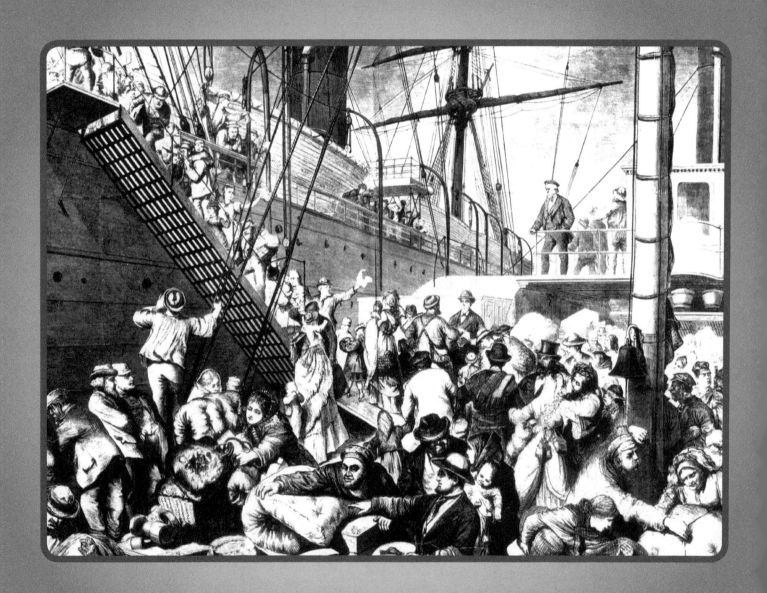

IRISH IMMIGRATION TO AMERICA

THE IRISH COME TO AMERICA

Irish people came early to the British colonies in North America, many as soldiers. There were so many in the Boston area by the 1730s that the Charitable Irish Society was formed there. New York and Philadelphia also had significant Irish populations from early in their history.

The first Irish to arrive were Protestants. The second great migration of Irish people were mainly Roman Catholics, driven to leave their country by the Potato Famine that started in 1845.

THE FAMINE MEMORIAL IN DUBLIN

ST. PATRICK'S DAY PARADE

THE START OF ST. PATRICK'S DAY

The first parade to mark Saint Patrick's Day was in Boston in 1762, although there had been feasts and other ways to mark the day in the city since 1737. This is earlier than any parade to mark the day even in Ireland! The marchers were mainly Irish soldiers serving in the British Army.

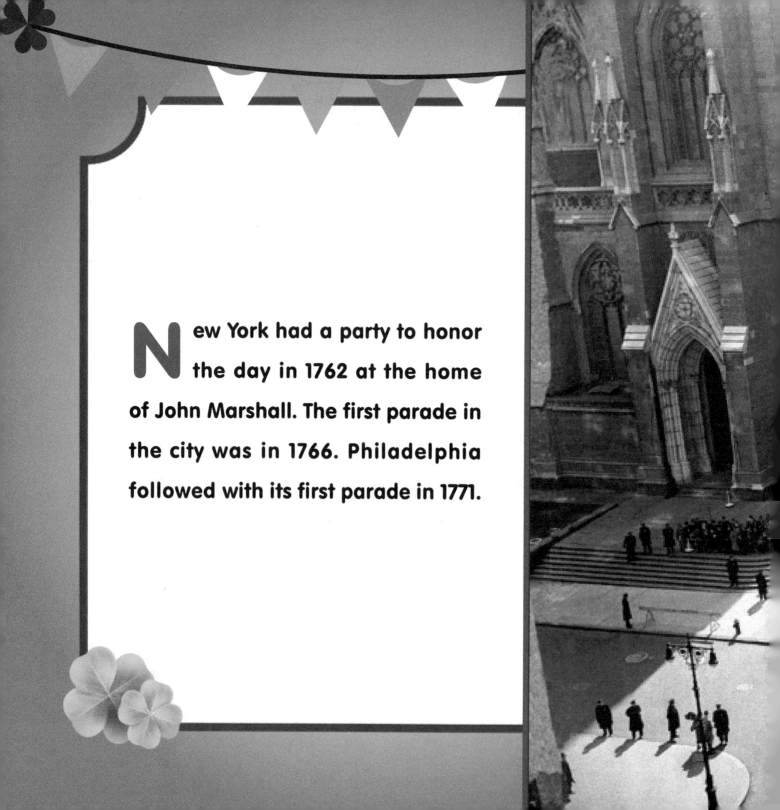

New York had a party to honor the day in 1762 at the home of John Marshall. The first parade in the city was in 1766. Philadelphia followed with its first parade in 1771.

ST. PATRICK'S DAY PARADE IN NEW YORK

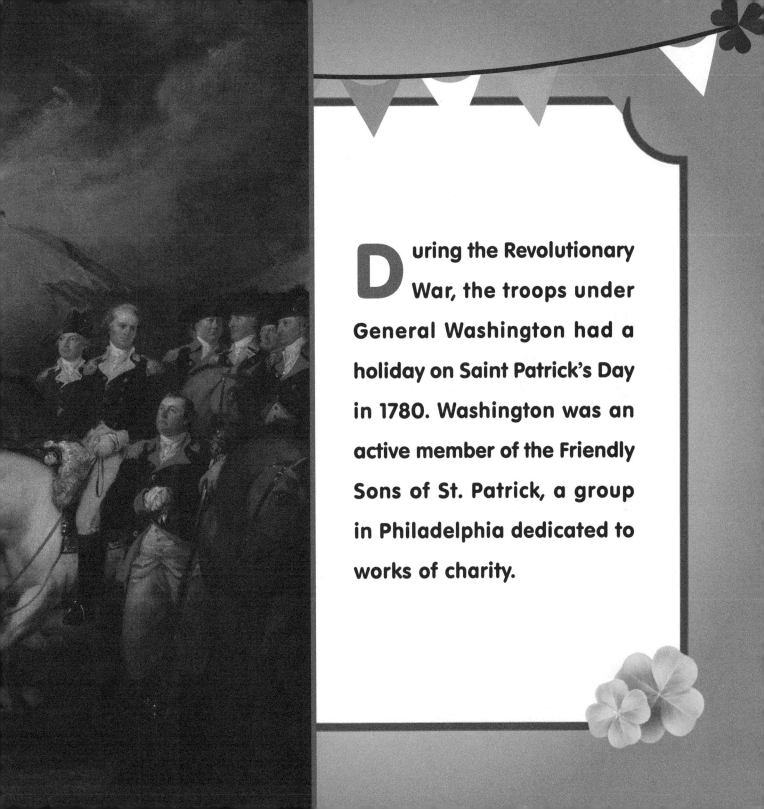

During the Revolutionary War, the troops under General Washington had a holiday on Saint Patrick's Day in 1780. Washington was an active member of the Friendly Sons of St. Patrick, a group in Philadelphia dedicated to works of charity.

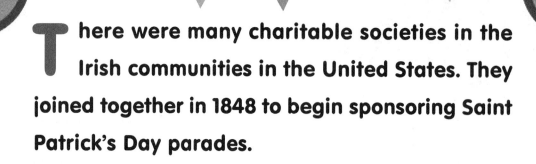

There were many charitable societies in the Irish communities in the United States. They joined together in 1848 to begin sponsoring Saint Patrick's Day parades.

ST. PATRICK'S DAY NEW YORK CITY 2013

The parade in New York City quickly became the largest annual parade in the United States, and one of the largest in the world.

Early celebrations of the day tended to focus on the works of the saint, and on homesickness for Ireland. From the middle of the nineteenth century, the parade and other activities on Saint Patrick's Day concentrated more and more on pride in being Irish, and on the contributions Irish people have made to American society.

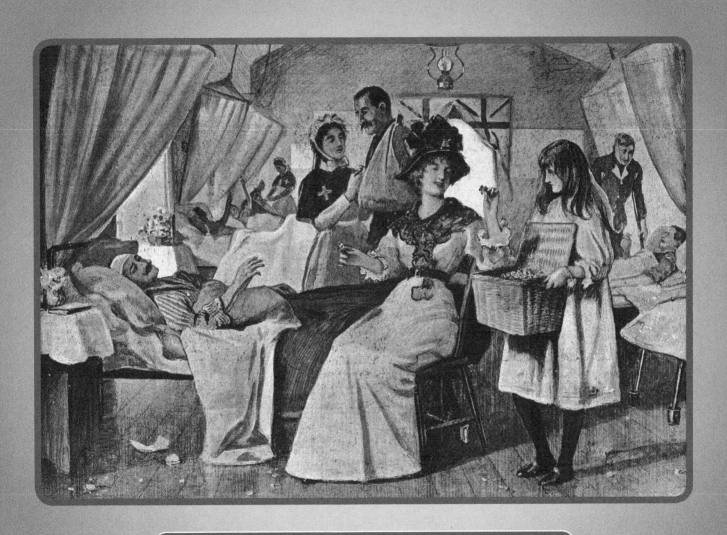

HOSPITAL WARD ON ST. PATRICK'S DAY

ST. PATRICK'S DAY IN SOUTH BOSTON

CELEBRATING THE DAY

Saint Patrick's Day is only a legal holiday in one county of Massachusetts, but it is observed all across the United States.

Since 1991, either the United States Congress or the President have issued a proclamation designating March as Irish-American heritage month. For most Irish-Americans, the holiday has both religious and national overtones. For Roman Catholics of Irish descent, celebrating Saint Patrick happens both in church and in the town. Since Saint Patrick's Day happens during the fasting season of Lent, and the Church allows celebration on the day, it is a welcome break!

The down-side of many celebrations over the years is that the holiday has been seen as a time when it is all right to drink a lot of alcohol. This plays into the caricature of Irish people as heavy drinkers, although getting drunk has nothing at all to do with Saint Patrick! Many cities are now taking steps to tone down the approval of public drunkenness and bad behavior that often follow from it.

GROUP OF MEN WITH BEERS

Here are some traditional events during Saint Patrick's Day in cities across the United States.

All over the country, people wear some *green clothing* to mark the day. In certain areas, the tradition is to pinch people who are not wearing green!

Savannah, Georgia started its celebrations in 1824. Events start around March 10 and build up to the great parade on March 17.

*S*eattle, Washington, and many other cities, paint a green stripe down the streets that the Saint Patrick's Day parade uses as its marching route.

Chicago, *Illinois* has been coloring its river green for the day, ever since an accidental discovery in 1962. Workers used a green dye to check for leaks in the sewer system, and the dye worked so well that it was decided to use it in the river.

At first, the city used over 100 pounds of vegetable dye each year, and the river stayed green for a week! Now much less dye is used, and the river returns to normal color after a few hours.

Indianapolis, Indiana and Savannah, Georgia dyes its central canal green, and Savannah, Georgia dyes the water in the city fountains downtown.

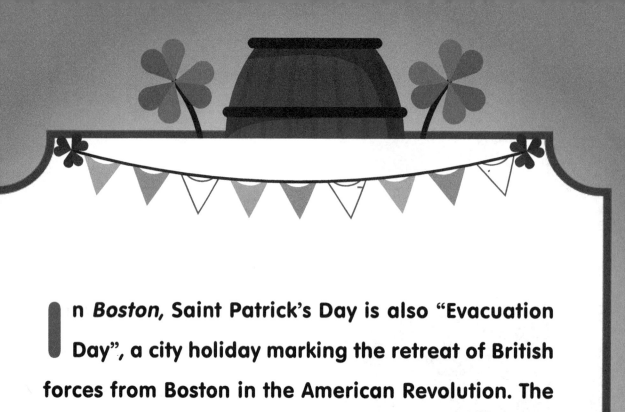

In *Boston*, Saint Patrick's Day is also "Evacuation Day", a city holiday marking the retreat of British forces from Boston in the American Revolution. The combination of holidays, and time off work, have helped boost participation in the parade and other events.

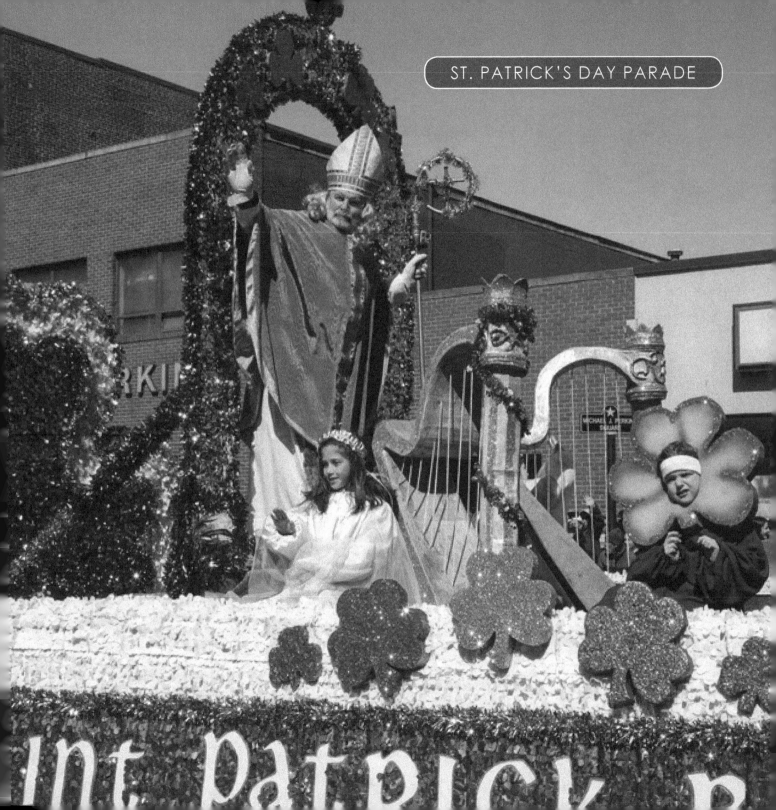

ST. PATRICK'S DAY MARATHON

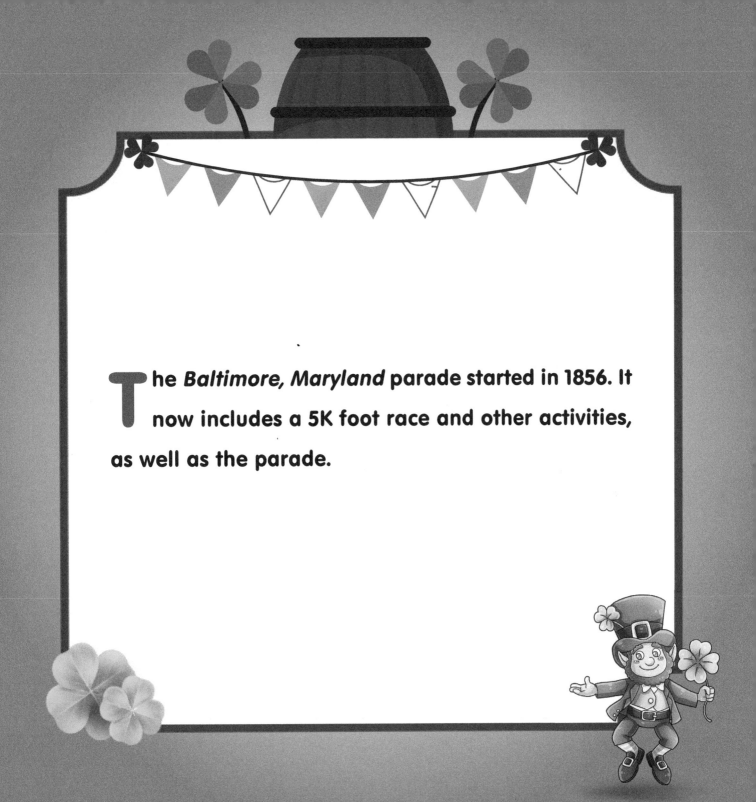

The *Baltimore, Maryland* parade started in 1856. It now includes a 5K foot race and other activities, as well as the parade.

A lot of Irish people moved to *Montana* to work in the mines. The normal population of *Butte*, the state's largest city, is about 40,000 people...but it doubles on Saint Patrick's Day as people come to the city from all around to take part in the festivities.

ST. PATRICK'S DAY, BUTTE
MONTANA (2007)

ST. PATRICK'S DAY, ALABAMA

*E*nterprise, *Alabama* claims to have the world's smallest Saint Patrick's Day parade! Each year, just one person marches one block from the courthouse to a monument nearby and back again. He or she wears festive clothing and carries a large Irish flag.

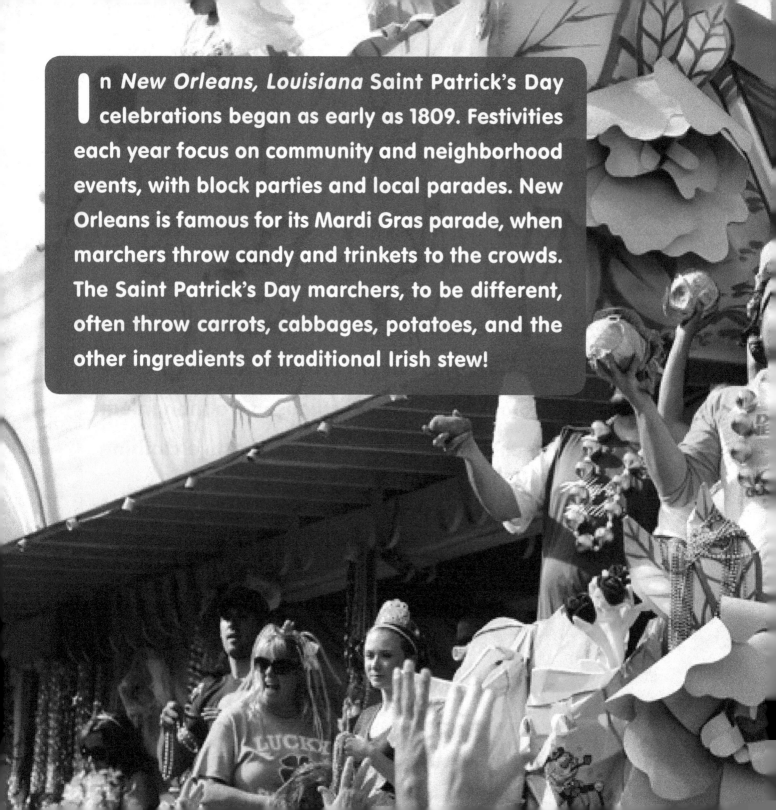

In *New Orleans, Louisiana* Saint Patrick's Day celebrations began as early as 1809. Festivities each year focus on community and neighborhood events, with block parties and local parades. New Orleans is famous for its Mardi Gras parade, when marchers throw candy and trinkets to the crowds. The Saint Patrick's Day marchers, to be different, often throw carrots, cabbages, potatoes, and the other ingredients of traditional Irish stew!

In *New York City*, more than 150,000 people march in each year's parade! The first group in the five-hour march is always a detachment of the 69th Infantry Regiment. Politicians of every ethnic background become "Irish for the day" and take part in the march.

In *Pittsburgh, Pennsylvania* the city shuts down for the day as hundreds of thousands of people attend the parade and other festivities. The first Saint Patrick's Day parade in the city took place in 1869. Highway bridges and tunnels are closed to cars as crowds use them to walk into the city. Almost 14 percent of the city's population identifies as Irish-American.

San Francisco, California has had a festival for Saint Patrick's Day since at least 1852. In the nineteenth century Irish Americans were the largest group in the city. In recent times that honor belongs to Chinese Americans, and a lot of Irish American families have moved to the suburbs. However, for Saint Patrick's Day, thousands of people flood back into the city to take part in or watch the parade, and to show off their green clothing.

ST. PATRICK'S DAY, SAN FRANCISCO

SHORECREST HIGH SCHOOL HIGHLANDERS
ST. PATRICK'S DAY PARADE

Seattle, *Washington* holds a parade that draws participants from all over the northwestern United States. The parade passes through the center of the city on the Saturday before Saint Patrick's Day; the day before, people take part in the "laying of the green", painting the green stripe down the middle of the parade route.

SAINT PATRICK'S DAY TOASTS

Saint Patrick's Day festivities often involve great feasts and a lot of drinking. Some of the beverages can seem a little unusual. In a lot of cities, there is a tradition of dyeing the beer green for the day!

CELEBRATING ST. PATRICK'S DAY
WITH GREEN BEER

People salute each other over their drinks with traditional toasts. Here are some phrases you may hear:

- May the roof above us never fall in, and may the friends beneath it never fall out.

- Here's to absent friends, and here's twice to absent enemies.

- May you be in heaven for a full half hour before the devil knows you're dead.

- May sorrow follow you all of your days—but never catch up!

- May your home always be too small to hold all of your friends.

REMEMBERING WHO WE ARE

Holidays are not just fun, but a chance to remember who we are and who we are becoming. Keeping alive cultural traditions helps make all of the United States stronger. We remember where our parents and ancestors came from, and what they have contributed to the development of the country.

Learn about other holidays, both in the United States and around the world, in Baby Professor books like *Why do the Chinese Have a Different New Year?*, *Happy Father's Day, Dad!*, and *Who Started the Labor Day Celebration?*

Visit

BABY PROFESSOR
EDUCATION KIDS

www.BabyProfessorBooks.com

to download Free Baby Professor eBooks
and view our catalog of new and exciting
Children's Books

CPSIA information can be obtained
at www.ICGtesting.com
Printed in the USA
LVHW062138040321
680651LV00037B/666